GOOD HOUSEKEEPING

SIMPLE HOUSEHOLD WISDOM

200+ EASY WAYS TO CLEAN & ORGANIZE YOUR HOME

EDITED BY SARA LYLE BOW

HEARST books

HEARST BOOKS

An Imprint of Sterling Publishing Co., Inc.
122 Fifth Avenue
New York, NY 10011

ISBN 978-1-61837-320-5

For information about custom editions, special sales, and premium and corporate purchases, please contact Sterling Special Sales at 800-805-5489 or specialsales@sterlingpublishing.com.

Manufactured in Singapore

2 4 6 8 10 9 7 5 3 1

sterlingpublishing.com

goodhousekeeping.com
Design by Susan Welt for gonzalez defino, ny

CONTENTS

CHAPTER 1
KEEP THINGS CLEAN | **4**

CHAPTER 2
BANISH CLUTTER! | **22**

CHAPTER 3
CARE FOR CLOTHES | **46**

CHAPTER 4
KITCHEN HACKS | **68**

CHAPTER 5
DECORATE IT YOURSELF | **88**

PHOTO CREDITS | 110

INDEX | 110

BEDDED BLISS

Keep your bedroom clutter-free by stationing adequate storage for your needs. Consider displaying your books on a coffee table instead of piled on the nightstand. A tiny bedside shelf helps keep necessities handy and within reach.

chapter

1

GOOD HOUSEKEEPING

KEEP THINGS CLEAN

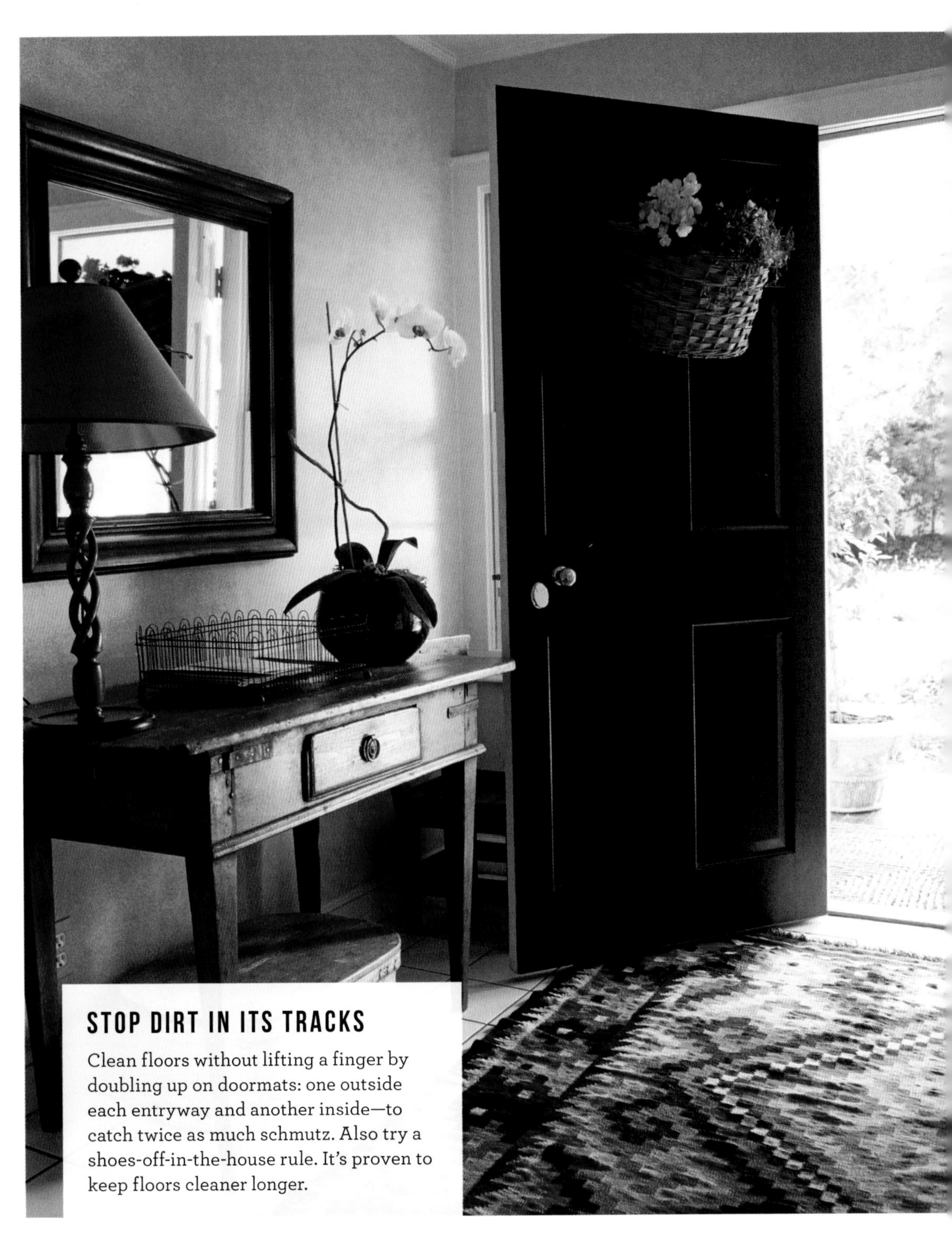

STOP DIRT IN ITS TRACKS

Clean floors without lifting a finger by doubling up on doormats: one outside each entryway and another inside—to catch twice as much schmutz. Also try a shoes-off-in-the-house rule. It's proven to keep floors cleaner longer.

CLEAR BRILLIANCE

The GH Institute–tested trick for spotless windows? Dust frames and sills first, then wash glass from side to side on one side and top to bottom on the other. If there are streaks, you can tell which side to re-do.

THROW IN THE TOWEL

They may not look dirty, but dish towels were deemed the most contaminated spot in the kitchen in a USDA-funded study. Change them out every couple of days, or even every day if you have a large family.

CLEAN SMARTER, NOT HARDER

Because how much do you *really* like doing it?

BE A TWO-TIMER

Forget trying to multitask. Better to use your time doing mini tasks during otherwise wasted minutes. Straighten a coat closet when your TV show goes to commercial, fold some laundry while on hold listening to call-center Muzak or unload the dishwasher as you wait for that pasta water to boil.

BUT STAY SINGLE-MINDED...

...when you're cleaning several rooms. Rather than tackling an entire room top to bottom, do one task from room to room. For instance, use a multipurpose spray on glass, metal and laminated or painted surfaces, then go back and polish wood furniture. You'll switch cloths and product containers less frequently—and finish faster.

USE LESS PRODUCT, NOT MORE

While it's tempting to spray down a window or mirror with glass cleaner, or spritz wood polish directly on furniture, don't. Instead, squirt solution on your cloth or sponge. This saves you product *and* effort—less wiping and, in the case of wood furniture, less dusting, since most polishes can leave a filmy buildup that attracts the pesky particles.

THAT'S GENIUS! Upcycle a **plastic or metal clothes hanger** to hold your paper towel roll as you clean room to room—first snip the hanger's crossbar in the center. Hang it on a knob to free up your hands and make it easier to pull off sheets.

TAKE COVER

No one is suggesting you cover your furniture with plastic like the parents in *My Big Fat Greek Wedding* (nor should you use Windex® to fix every ailment!). But when it comes to taking care of your stuff—and cleaning less—prevention is key. Invest in some stylish slipcovers for upholstered pieces. White matches everything and is simple to bleach.

FRESHEN FAST!

Grab these everyday items to zap odors on the double.

MAKE LEMON AID

Lemons smell clean, so try this: Cut one in half, put the pieces in a microwave-safe bowl with water to cover and heat on High for two to three minutes. While you enjoy the citrus scent, the steam softens hardened splatters inside the oven. Then, grind the fruit in the garbage disposal to eliminate any mustiness and greasy gunk.

KNOW YOUR JOE

It's no wonder perfume departments often display little bowls of coffee beans or fresh grinds—one big sniff quickly rids your nostrils of lingering aromas. Employ the same tactic in your fridge or freezer, the mudroom, on a shelf in your teenager's closet or anyplace that gets overly ripe.

GOOD PETKEEPING

Fur everywhere? Odor overwhelming? Puddles multiplying? Try these tricks to minimize Mr. Whiskers' mess.

DE-STINK your dog between baths: Lightly sprinkle her fur with baking soda, rub it in and then brush it out.

DE-FUZZ upholstery, drapes and even clothes with the easy-to-grip Scotch-Brite® Upholstery Pet Hair Remover. Or go low-tech and dampen clean rubber gloves to collect the fur.

UNDO STAINS (of the bodily fluid kind) with Bissell's pet stain removers. No time to shop? Try the DIY method on the right.

PREVENT SPILLS with an inexpensive rubber pet placemat that stops bowls from sliding and protects floors from food and water splatters.

DIY PET URINE DETERRENTS

Your hydrangeas shouldn't double as a litter box. Combine **used coffee grounds and orange peels** to create a pungent mixture. Sprinkle it on top of your soil, and the neighbor's cat won't go near the odor.

As for those yellow urine patches, the only way to prevent them is to curb your dog. If you catch him (or another pup) lifting his leg on the grass, quickly **douse the spot with a hose.** Existing yellow patches may need reseeding.

Pet relieved himself *indoors*? Try this GH Institute method to get urine out of carpet: Mix 1 Tbsp. of liquid hand dishwashing detergent and 1 Tbsp. of white vinegar with 2 cups of warm water. Using a clean white cloth, sponge the stain with the solution. Blot until the liquid is absorbed. If the stain remains, use an eyedropper to apply hydrogen peroxide, and then add a drop or two of ammonia (not on silk or wool). Sponge with cold water and blot dry.

SPEED CLEANING

Go on, be lazy, er, strategic! You'll save time by putting off these tasks.

CLEANING OUT THE FRIDGE

Why bother doing it before trash day? Or, if you miss the garbage truck, wait to toss spoiled or expired food until the day you go grocery shopping. That way, you'll make room for incoming food, have a better idea of what items you need to restock *and* avoid having stinky leftovers hanging out in your trash bin for too long.

DUSTING THE BATHROOM

The time to do it: when you're changing out your used hand towel or towels. Then, you can use the terry cloth, preferably damp, to wipe down those dusty surfaces (e.g., counter and toilet tops—and anything on top of them; baseboards). This quick once-over will cut down on your need to deep clean more frequently.

WASHING DISHES BEFORE YOU PUT THEM IN THE MACHINE

Yes, you should scrape any food scraps into the garbage, but don't bother handwashing or even rinsing your dishes before you put them in the dishwasher. Research shows that it doesn't get your dishes any cleaner—and our GH Institute experts agree—as long as you don't let dishes sit before washing.

FAMILY MATTERS

How to split up chores evenly? Set aside an hour or two each week for cleaning. Write tasks on slips of paper and put them in bowls according to difficulty. Have each family member choose from the appropriate bowl—then have the crew get to work!

16 MINUTES TO A CLEAN HOUSE

Your place is a mess, and guests are on their way. Don't. Freak. Out. Just use this 4-step plan to have a presentable pad in minutes.

1 **START WITH THE BATHROOM.** Use an all-purpose cleaning wipe to clean the sink, countertops and toilet top. Clean the mirror and fixtures, straighten the shower curtain and hang fresh towels. *Time: 4 minutes.*

2 **MOVE ON TO THE KITCHEN.** Hide dirty dishes and cookware in the dishwasher if empty; if not, hide them in the oven. Use a wipe to clean the counters. *Time: 2½ minutes.*

3 **DECLUTTER AND DUST THE LIVING SPACES.** Put newspapers, magazines, shoes and other clutter into a shopping bag or laundry basket, then hide the bag or basket in a bedroom or closet—preferably one you use often, so it isn't forgotten. *Time: 4½ minutes.*

4 **END WITH THE FLOORS.** Vacuum main traffic areas and living spaces, including carpets and bare floors, with a rechargeable stick vac. Store the vac, and greet your company! *Time: 5 minutes.*

IF YOU RUN OUT OF...

WINDOW CLEANER

Swap in 2 Tbsp. non-sudsy ammonia mixed with 1 quart (4 cups) water in a spray bottle.

LAUNDRY STAIN REMOVER

Swap in liquid dish soap or a few drops of hydrogen peroxide, which works like color-safe bleach.

SHOWER CLEANER

Swap in baking soda sprinkled on a damp sponge or a scrub brush.

GENTLE FABRIC DETERGENT

Swap in mild shampoo (and hand-wash in cool water in the sink).

TOILET BOWL CLEANER

Swap in 1 cup chlorine bleach. Pour into the bowl, swish clean with a brush, let sit 10 minutes and flush.

THE DON'T LIST

Before diving in, review these rules so you won't damage surfaces or fabrics.

1 DON'T USE VINEGAR ON STONE COUNTERS. It can etch and mar materials like granite. Use a mild stone cleaner, like Granite Gold®, instead.

2 DON'T MIX BLEACH WITH AMMONIA. Nor with ammonia-containing products, such as some window cleaners. When combined, they produce gas that can constrict breathing.

3 DON'T TRY BLEACH TO REMOVE RUST. It'll actually set the stain. Use a specially formulated rust-stain remover, such as GH-tested Whink®.

4 **DON'T WASH YOUR CAR WITH DISH SOAP.** It's harsher on the car's paint than a car wash. GH Institute pick: Simple Green® Car Wash.

5 **DON'T CLEAN STONE FLOORS WITH VINEGAR.** Just like countertops, the natural stone in your bathroom doesn't take kindly to acidic cleaners, like vinegar and lemon. Avoid ammonia, too, and stick to cleaning with special stone soap, or dish detergent and water.

6 **DON'T USE LAUNDRY STAIN REMOVER ON CARPETS.** It can leave a sticky residue that's a magnet for dirt. Go with a spray formulated for carpets.

7 **DON'T DOUSE YOUR CARPET TO REMOVE A FRESH STAIN.** Oversaturating the stain with water can damage the fibers, and excess moisture can leak through to the rug pad and flooring, where it can get trapped. Instead, employ the blot method for lifting stains. Lightly spritz with water to rinse (followed by more blotting with a clean, dry paper towel or cloth).

TAKE CARE OF YOUR TOOLS

Unless you clean your cleaning gear—and toss expired products—you could be pushing around grime and germs, or simply wasting your time. Here's how to handle it all.

BROOM
Vacuum the head with a handheld attachment or swish it in warm, soapy water; let dry, head down.

VACUUM
Empty the dirt receptacle after every couple of uses or replace the disposable bag before it's three-quarters full. Also change or wash the filters regularly.

MOP
Rinse or wash the strings, sponge or microfiber pad and squeeze out excess water. Hang the mop by its handle or stand it upside down to dry. Most strip and microfiber mop heads are removable and machine washable, too.

KITCHEN SPONGE
Once a week, soak the sponge for five minutes in a solution of 1½ Tbsp. chlorine bleach in 2 cups water. Launder any used cleaning rags weekly—or more frequently if needed.

WRITE ON YOUR WALLS

A bold chalkboard-painted accent wall in the kitchen is an eye-catching spot to jot down a daily to-do list or display a curated selection of your kids' art. Use adhesive-backed bulldog clips to hang their masterpieces.

chapter

2

GOOD HOUSEKEEPING

BANISH CLUTTER!

SHOW SOME PERSONALITY

Organizing vessels don't have to be boring. Make the flea market or consignment shop your best friend, and find vintage suitcases, picnic baskets, trunks and more to hold items you want handy but tucked out of sight.

SWANEE

SOLVE THE LINEN CLOSET

Adopt these mess-taming tips: Store off-season bedding in bins. To retain their fluff, keep out pillows, comforters or any down-filled items, or only vacuum-seal them about 50 percent. Place dividers between towel piles and sheet sets, separated by bathroom or bedroom (master, guests, kids).

ANTI-WRINKLE ADVICE

The trick to repurposing gift bags? Keep them wrinkle-free. Rather than throwing them in a pile in your closet, use a file organizer to stand them upright. To revive wrinkled fabric ribbons: Iron them on low heat (you may need a spritz of water).

BE A WRAP STAR

If you give a lot of gifts throughout the year, do *yourself* a favor and create a station for wrapping presents. Musts: a tall vessel to hold rolls of specialty papers (no-tearing tip: Secure paper with loops cut from old tights) as well as rods to suspend rolls of frequently used wraps and ribbon.

ORGANIZING TRICKS THAT WORK

Try these simple solutions for real results. Your house will thank you.

WORK WITH YOUR HABITS

Does your husband dump out his pockets on the dresser every night? Don't fight it. Instead, set a decorative dish on top and a wastebasket below—and let him sort out what to keep and what to trash each evening. Similarly, if you like to try on or take off jewelry in the bathroom but then forget to put it away, place a small bowl on the counter to hold pieces. Once a receptacle is full, deal with its contents.

DEVELOP NEW ONES

The organizer's maxim: A place for everything and everything in its place. Assign spots for easily misplaced items, such as a hook by the back door for car keys, a tray on the coffee table for TV remotes or a holder for your reading glasses by the bed. Commit to returning things to their places, and you'll soon spend less time looking for stuff that's "lost."

STREAMLINE FURNITURE

With too many chairs or tables, even the most spacious room can look like an episode of *Hoarders*. To cut down on visual clutter and ease traffic flow, move out excess pieces. When investing in new furniture, focus on function *then* form. A coffee table or nightstand, for instance, should have at least one drawer, shelf or cabinet to keep items contained.

THAT'S GENIUS! The humble **shoebox** is often just the thing to hold, well, just about anything. Plus, it's free! Make sure to label what's inside, if you're putting the box away for storage. Or wrap the box and lid separately with decorative paper and leave it on display.

DECANT TO SAVE SPACE

Remove some TP, cotton balls and cotton swabs from the original packaging—and put them into reusable containers—to expand valuable inches in the bathroom vanity. Likewise, decant oversized bottles of mouthwash or pump (not aerosol) hair product into smaller vessels, so that they fit in the medicine cabinet or vanity, too.

PRACTICE SHELF PRESERVATION

Here's a novel idea: Cover the backs of bookcases with decorative paper, or paint the insides a poppy hue, and you'll be more inclined to show them off—and less likely to cover them up with clutter. Today's self-adhesive wallpaper makes it a snap to peel and stick.

RECLAIM THE JUNK DRAWER

It's time for it to hold its own! (You know, minus the clutter.)

1 Group the contents into categories (e.g., paper clips, rubber bands, coins, nails and screws), then relocate items that belong elsewhere, such as screwdrivers (toolbox) and bandages (medicine cabinet).

2 Eliminate duplicates or non-working items (locks without keys, broken toys). If you don't already have one, start a change jar so that you can cash in on its contents.

3 To finish, sort what's left into utensil dividers or small gift boxes. Order restored!

PREVENT PAPER CLUTTER

Cut those piles down to size with these smart tips.

MAKE AN ENTRANCE

The first step to eliminating paper clutter? Bar it at the door. Subject every piece of paper that comes into your house to the "two Fs" test: If you can't file or frame it, out it goes. Also try positioning two bins in or near the foyer—one for recycling and one for shredding—so that it's easier to stay on top of those tasks.

CLEAR THE DECK

Reclaim your out-of-control desktop: Take everything off its surface and replace the essentials. Then hang up daily-use references (e.g., a calendar) for speedy review. Organize what's left for storage: in drawers or cabinets or on shelves (if needed, corral items in dividers for faster scan-and-grab).

ELIMINATE PAPER—
DIGITALLY!

CATALOG CHOICE

Visit catalogchoice.org to cancel unsolicited catalogs or download the free Catalog Spree (iOS) for digital versions of those you do want.

COZI

Want to streamline your family's schedules? Try Cozi, a free web service that helps you manage multiple calendars and lists as well as send messages and reminders directly to your family members' phones or email. Each person is assigned a color on the calendar, so you can easily reference who's going where and when.

TURBOSCAN

TurboScan Pro lets you scan and send a plethora of things: multipage documents, receipts for tax purposes, business cards for work. Meaning? You can toss the actual pieces of paper.

BEAT BUILDUP

Block off a half hour on your calendar once a month to clear out old catalogs, magazines and notes before they get out of hand.

TEAR IT UP!

Thwart would-be identity thieves by turning important docs into confetti. When shopping for a shredder, look for features that prevent paper jams caused by "overfeeding," shut off automatically if the paper slot is touched (a must for a home office prone to pop-ins from kids or pets), and allow you to easily see when it needs emptying.

ALWAYS **SHRED** THESE

You may be tempted to shred everything—or nothing. To be safe, don't skip the following five types of documents.

• Anything you don't need that lists your Social Security number

• Unsolicited credit card offers

• Credit card statements and checks you no longer need

• Bank statements, brokerage, and mutual fund statements you no longer need

• Insurance claim offers you no longer need

BEFORE YOU BUY

Check the shred capacity before buying—it tells you how much your machine can handle before jamming. We recommend a sheet or two less than that.

BEFORE YOU SHRED

Line your bin with a shredder bag to make trash disposal quick and easy.

LOOK UP!

Use your walls, doors and other vertical surfaces to eke out as much storage space as possible.

GO ALL THE WAY

No one says you have to end your shelving before it reaches the ceiling, if that's what you desire—or that's how much stuff you need to stock. (Perk: It can make your ceilings look taller.) Buy or build add-on shelves for existing bookcases, and make sure to mount the unit to the wall.

OPEN POSSIBILITIES

Kitchen drawer jammed with menus? Bathroom counter a tangle of hair tools? Disposable shopping bags stashed around the house? Check *inside* your cabinets—there's usually space to mount or hang specialty holders on the door, such as see-through pocket folders, a rack for saucepan lids or a plastic bag dispenser for under the kitchen sink.

BE A-DOOR-ABLE

Hanging shoe organizers are meant for shoes—but don't let that stop you! Inside a closet in your kid's room, they hold toys and other miscellany. Within an entryway closet, their pockets are perfect receptacles for small umbrellas, travel tissue packs, extra packs of chewing gum or other things you need when you're running out the door.

GOTTA HAVE 'EM! STORAGE STANDOUTS

These organizing finds are clever and chic. Just like you.

STYLISH BASKETS

Roomy baskets can jazz up your décor while helping you manage messiness. If you're looking to store holders on shelves, square or rectangular shapes fit better than round ones.

WALL HOOKS

Hooks 101: Make sure you have enough to do the job, whether it's to hang ties in the bedroom or towels in the bath. If you have too few (or ones that aren't sturdy enough), they'll be overrun and, ultimately, underused.

WHEELED BOXES

These plastic wonders will let you take back the space under your beds currently inhabited by dust bunnies.

HANDLED TRAYS

A smart way to corral items in clutter-prone zones (the kitchen counter, a foyer table): sleek trays that can be picked up—to relocate or repurpose—in a pinch.

LAZY SUSANS

Spinning organizers make the most of cramped cabinets. Look for split-level versions that let you stash twice the stuff!

MULTIFUNCTION FURNITURE

The beauty of lidded ottomans? Cheery stools like this one hold their contents *plus* whatever you place on top, be it a tray for drinks or your backside.

MAKE OVER THE MUDROOM

Put clutter in its place (read: leave it in the entryway) with these genius ideas.

SEAT YOURSELF

Discourage disorganization with a pretty pillow-topped bench—it's the ideal place to sit and remove muddy boots or rip open mail. Non-lidded bins and baskets make it easy to toss in or pull out (non-wet) shoes, scarves, pet gear and more.

DOUBLE HOOKS

Choose coat hooks that have both top and bottom sections for extra spots to hang gear. Have young kids? Paint each a different color so they know which is theirs. Wicker picnic and fishing baskets transform mudroom chaos into calm.

MAXIMIZE CLOTHES QUARTERS

Whether you have an entryway closet or freestanding cabinets, don't skimp on sturdy hangers—basic metal hangers will bend under the weight of heavier coats. Informal jackets can hang on hooks or pegs.

TUCK IT IN

Create a mini mudroom under your stairs. Narrow, wall-mounted shelves are a sleek spot for holding shoes and bags. A perfectly proportioned umbrella stand sits neatly against the wall. (Tip: The best stands allow for air circulation, such as wicker, mesh, slatted or open-sided styles.)

HOOK, DON'T HEAP

Avoid doubling up items on hooks, pegs or knobs. Otherwise, damp jackets won't dry well and may become funky smelling. See page 39 for a stylish solution.

GET AROUND

Take your organizing attempts from eyesore to artful by arranging your storage solution—like these drum-shaped catchalls—into a geometric display. Sturdy hatboxes (minus the lids) will produce a similar effect.

ORGANIZING RULES OF THUMB

Practice these three lessons, and you'll be an organizing expert in no time.

1 **PUT ITEMS WITHIN REACH.** Constantly pulling out a step stool or stooping over to retrieve things? Always have to reach around or rifle through stuff to find what you need? Consider this an intervention. The most accessible storage is located in the space between your shoulders and knees. So, place items you use most often in this region—and position the things you use all the time in the *front* of the drawer, cabinet or shelf.

2 **GROUP LIKE WITH LIKE.** Example: Put all of the cooking utensils in one pottery container adjacent to the stove. When it comes to finding a place for seasonal items—like lawn furniture, sports equipment or holiday decorations—store them in the same area (e.g., attic, basement, garage or garden shed). That way, since you're rotating stuff in and out, there will always be a bit of space (think snow skis replacing water skis).

3 LABEL IT— OR NOT. If you're using see-through bins or canisters, labels are usually optional. The exceptions: if you have a lot of identical vessels (for, say, craft supplies or shoes) or if it might cue family members or guests where items go. For opaque holders (file folders, canvas boxes) or seldom-accessed seasonal or special occasion storage, labels save you search time. Trust us.

DOES IT PAY TO HIRE A PRO?

TO ORGANIZE YOUR HOUSE

Calling in an expert to help organize your home can pay off for years to come, particularly if you're time pressed or overwhelmed by decluttering to-dos.

Find a qualified pro on the National Association of Productivity & Organizing Professionals' site (**napo.net**). Hourly or project-based fees vary widely, though NAPO recommends *not* hiring based on price alone. "Focus on finding an organizer with a personality and skill set that matches your needs," it instructs. The downside to outsourcing? If you and your family can't or don't stick with the new system, it can be a waste of money.

If you simply need a fresh perspective on what to purge from a specific closet or room, invite over a decisive friend to provide moral support.

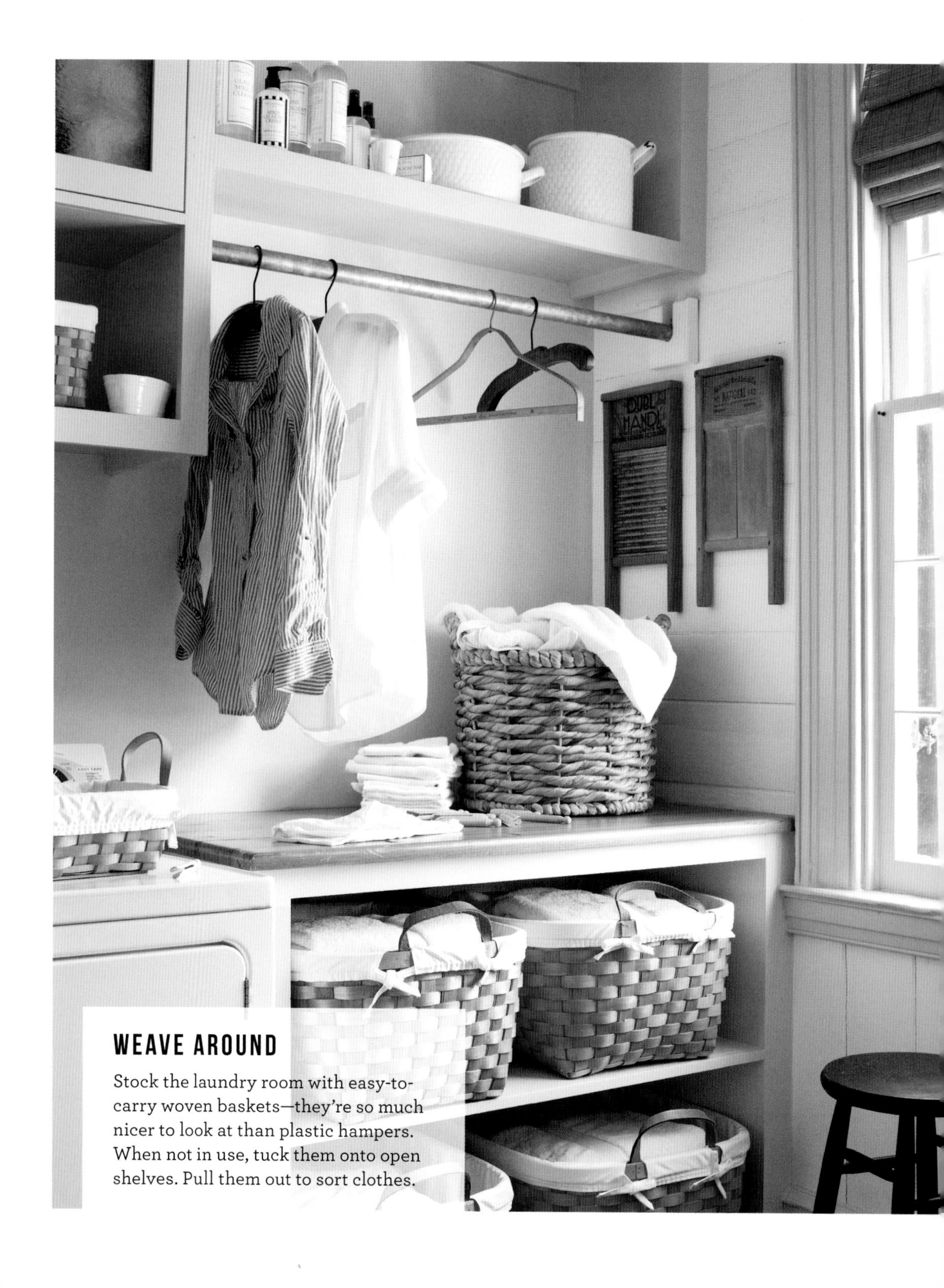

WEAVE AROUND

Stock the laundry room with easy-to-carry woven baskets—they're so much nicer to look at than plastic hampers. When not in use, tuck them onto open shelves. Pull them out to sort clothes.

chapter

3

GOOD HOUSEKEEPING

CARE FOR CLOTHES

DRESS FOR SUCCESS

Mount a hook outside your closet, or hang one over the door, and each night pull out an outfit to wear the next day. Even if your closet stays impenetrable, your a.m. routine will be simpler—and you'll start the day in style.

KEEP VS. TOSS

Toss scented drawer liners and sachets, whose oils can stain your lingerie. Instead, tuck in an empty bottle of your favorite perfume. Wrap it in a handkerchief to ensure that it doesn't give off anything but a hint of scent.

DIVIDE TO CONQUER

To instill some undergarment order, edit out tattered, ill-fitting or uncomfortable items (and be honest—you know you hate wearing that scratchy lace bra). Use inexpensive drawer dividers to give everything a place.

LIGHTEN UP YOUR LAUNDRY LOAD

Doing the wash will always be a chore. These expert tips make it feel a little less so.

DEAL WITH IT NOW

To make sure clothes aren't worse for the wear when they come *out* of the washer, first close zippers, hooks and snaps and tie straps and strings. Empty those pockets, too. Place a rail with clips or a small vessel nearby to hold anything you retrieve.

DEAL WITH IT LATER

When you spill coffee on your favorite blouse, there's no time to remove a fresh stain before work. So try a pre-treater that's safe to use up to several days before you wash, such as Shout® Advanced Ultra Gel Brush, which topped GH Institute tests.

AVOID THE HASSLE

Sort clothing *before* you reach the laundry room. There's no point in dragging it all there only to discover you don't have enough for, say, a full load of darks. And remember to keep items that shed (e.g., towels, sweaters, anything fleece or chenille) away from garments that attract lint, such as knits, synthetic fabrics and corduroy pants.

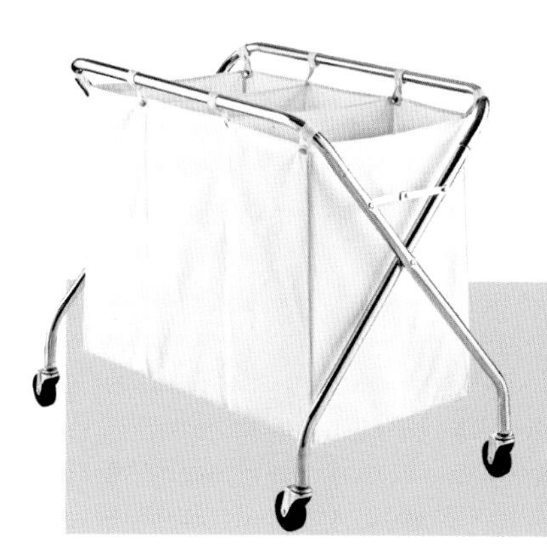

FAMILY MATTERS

Speed up the laundry-sorting process: Ask the family to pitch in. Opt for divided hampers for lights and darks, or go with separate baskets or bins for "delicates" and "everything else."

DOVETAIL YOUR TO-DOS

To save time and reduce fading, do "machine-wash warm" and "cold" loads together in cold water. Also, choose the shortest wash cycle—after all, once your clothes are clean, they're clean.

SET YOUR LINENS FREE

This may sound like extra work, but when drying large items like sheets and comforters, you'll want to frequently stop and readjust the load. Otherwise, the linens dry unevenly or may become balled up. (Dryers with drums that reverse-tumble throughout the cycle readjust automatically.)

ALL DRIED OUT

The nuts and bolts of getting the most out of your dryer.

LET THE MACHINE DO THE WORK

Use your dryer's automatic cycle. The sensors detect a load's moisture and stop the tumbling when contents are dry. No auto option? A half hour is usually plenty for a light load.

DON'T DOUBLE UP ON DRYING

If you mix towels or sweatshirts with lightweight garments, the latter will get overly dried while the heavier ones play catch-up. Drying two separate loads saves time overall.

HOW TO IRON LESS

Take garments out of the dryer before they're completely dry. Give them a good shake, and hang clothes on round shouldered hangers—unless they're better off folded (see page 61 for details). If that's the case, lay them flat to dry.

USE YOUR KNIT WITS

To avoid extra wrinkles, make sure the dryer isn't overloaded—cramming creates creases. Also, choose a slower spin speed on the washer (so wrinkles on clothes aren't set in) and a lower dryer temperature. Remove knits promptly when the dryer stops.

DEAL WITH DELICATES

Give your lingerie and "fancy" clothes the care they deserve. Slash dry-cleaning costs while you're at it!

PROTECT YOUR UNDIES & BRAS

Really want to extend the life of your bras and underwear? Zip them up in a mesh delicates bag before machine washing in cold water; also select the most gentle cycle. This will keep the elastic in better shape longer.

HANG THEM UP

Avoid putting bras in the dryer—heat can wreak havoc on their fibers. Smooth out lumps or dents in padded cups. Then, drape bras over coat hangers (or lay flat) to dry.

PRESS DELICATES WITH A CLOTH

Good to know: If you top your lacy or embellished blouse with a handkerchief or clean dish towel and set the iron's temp to match the fabric's most fragile fiber (e.g., nylon, silk), there's no need to go around the delicate or decorated areas.

GET KITTED OUT

Sewing box essentials: buttons, needles in different sizes, sharp scissors, spools of thread in a variety of colors (cotton-covered polyester and 100-percent polyester are all-purpose types), straight and safety pins, a tape measure and a thimble.

ON THE MEND

Do damage control: These simple DIY solutions will give your tattered clothes new life.

PILLING Grab an emery board or a dry scrubber sponge, and lightly rub over the pills to remove them. This is safer on fabrics than "snipping off" pills.

SWEATER PULLS Turn the sweater inside out and, using a crochet hook or blunt needle, carefully pull the snag through to the backside of the fabric. Gently tug or smooth both sides of the yarn loop.

FALLEN HEMS Skip sewing and use fusible web tape. Cut a piece to the length of the fallen hem. Sandwich it between the fabric layers and press the fabric with an iron and set it to the appropriate temperature. Truly desperate? Try duct tape to secure a hem in a pinch.

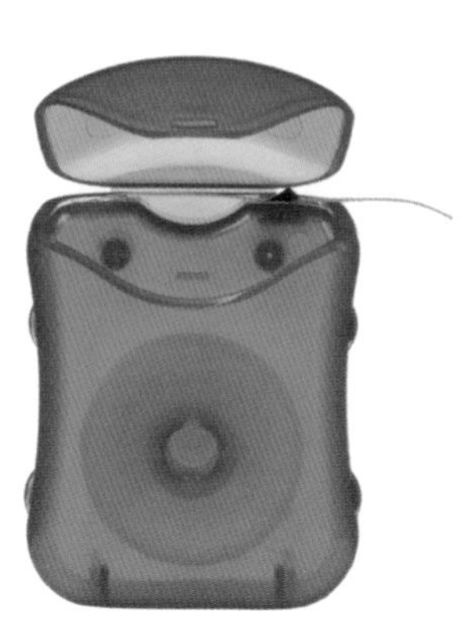

LOOSE OR LOST BUTTON You're better off watching YouTube™ for a how-to-sew-on-a-button video. But here's a GH Institute-approved tip: Use monofilament fishing line to secure a button on heavy coat and jacket materials (velvet, wool, denim) *or* try unwaxed unflavored dental floss.

END CLOSET CHAOS

Because you shouldn't dread opening that door or drawer.

FIRST THINGS FIRST

The best way to conquer clothes clutter: Hold your own once-a-year fashion show. Empty the closet, and try on each garment in front of a full-length mirror. Does it fit? With what outfits and on what occasions will you wear it? Does it need mending? Separate pieces into four piles: keep, mend, donate, throw away. Follow the same steps for shoes. Now you can start organizing the keepers.

DITCH THE DOOR

Once your closet is organized, if it's still cramped inside, consider taking off the doors and hanging curtains instead. Not only will it give bulkier items a little more room to breathe, it can save you square footage, if the doors aren't pocket style. Bonus: Curtains give your bedroom a soft, relaxed look.

TO HANG OR TO FOLD?

The way you hang your clothes can make a big difference in a) whether you have to dewrinkle them and b) how long they'll stay in good condition. For instance, fold trousers along the crease and double them over the hanger bar, and hang skirts by their loops to avoid unwanted fold marks and stretching. When it comes to stretchy materials like knit or beaded garments, however, avoid hanging them at all—gravity is not your friend; the clothes will lose their shape. Instead, roll thin knits, just as you would when packing for a trip, and fold heavy or bulky ones. Fold and store beaded items flat.

DOES IT PAY TO HIRE A PRO?

TO INSTALL CUSTOM CLOSETS

If you've got the extra cash, by all means, have the Container Store® install its sleek **Elfa®** system (for an additional 30 percent of your total purchase), or call in a company like **California Closets®** to alleviate your storage concerns. The results—being able to quickly locate both of your black pumps on a harried morning—may be priceless.

If your budget is more modest, take heart: The DIY systems on the market start around $300 and can be installed by mere mortals. Ones by **ClosetMaid®**—particularly the Selectives® and Shelftrack® lines—have done well in GH Institute observations of consumers assembling the systems. Just know, there may be some trial and error, and you should probably pick up a nice bottle of wine to celebrate with when you're all done. And partner up! Most systems require four hands!

DOUBLE YOUR (HANGING) PLEASURE

Many homebuilders default to "1R1S" or "one rod, one shelf" in closets, while most people (in this century at least!) don't have a wardrobe of only long dresses and coats. If you wear more separates, try installing a second clothing rod to maximize your hanging space. For a quick fix, buy a rod that hangs off the top one. You can set the width and height for a custom fit.

CASH IN!

TURN OLD CLOTHES INTO $$$

If you're so over those once-coveted Stuart Weitzman® boots (hey, fashion is fickle), it may be time to shop your closet.

POSHMARK®, a free mobile app, lets stylish types see and buy your treasures on the fly. Create listings by snapping pics with your smartphone of items you want to sell. Poshmark takes 20 percent off your price, and the buyer pays for shipping.

TRADESY®, a digital buy-and-sell marketplace, features both high-end (Alexander Wang®, Gucci®) and brand-name (J. Crew®, Zara®) labels. Designer duds usually go for 65 percent off retail; other clothes, 70 to 75 percent off. The site takes just 9 percent.

PLATO'S CLOSET® is a hip resale shop (with about 400 locations across the United States) that buys teens' and 20-somethings' clothes—typically stuff that's been in stores within the past 12 to 18 months.

THREDUP®, an online consignment shop, sends you a Clean Out Bag to fill with clothes and ship back, postage paid. Within a month, they'll let you know what they'll buy and for how much; you earn up to 80 percent of the selling price (they accept kids' clothes, too).

TOP-DOLLAR TRICK

When you post, include several photos showing front, back and side views—even of the interior of a handbag and the soles of shoes. Note anything unique, such as a blazer's silk lining.

SWAP SMART

When it comes to storing your seasonal clothes, don't save what you won't use. If you find that there are pieces that you haven't worn all winter or summer, donate them to charity. Chances are you won't wear them next year either.

DITCH THE MOTHBALLS

The traditional method of mothproofing winter wear in storage is on the outs. Experts say mothballs, which contain pesticides, can irritate eyes and skin and even affect the nervous system and liver. Try these safer ways to protect your cardigans.

CLEAN FIRST. Food and sweat stains are magnets for moths. Launder washables or dry-clean clothes before storing. Make sure laundered items are fully dry.

SEAL IN AIRTIGHT CONTAINERS. This keeps out moths *and* moisture, which can lead to mold. Try vacuum-sealed bags.

DON'T RELY ONLY ON CEDAR. The wood's oils may zap small larvae, but not large larvae or adult moths. Cedar lost its scent? Sand the wood to get it back.

DEAL WITH MOTHS. If you find them, move everything out and vacuum the carpet, walls and baseboards well (and toss the vacuum bag and dirt afterward). Scrub shelves and walls, then clean and store clothes properly.

BAG BASICS

Corral purses, wraps, etc., in a hanging bin with upward-slanting compartments so that items stay put, or along a shelf with dividers to stop totes from toppling over. Tuck in handbag handles to prevent damage. Hook belts and thin scarves onto separated hangers, or roll them and stow in a drawer or a bin.

DON'T FORGET THE ACCESSORIES!

They can really make an outfit. Here's how to wrangle bags, shoes, jewelry and more.

FILE THEM IN A CONVERTIBLE SHOE RACK like Lynk®'s 15-pair style, which can be built vertically or horizontally to best suit your space.

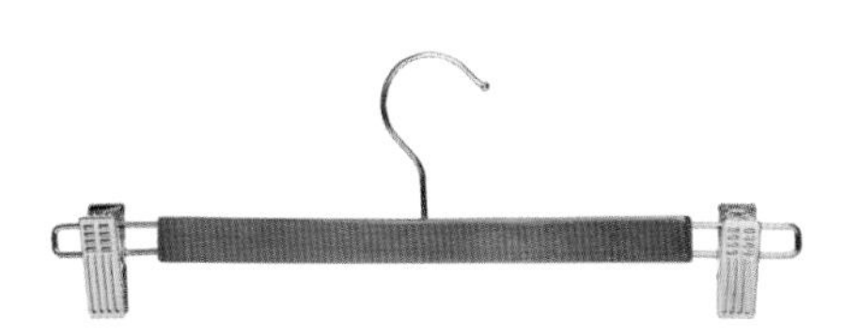

CLIP THEM UP. Even if you already have an over-the-door shoe organizer, it isn't always ideal for tall boots. Instead, attach boots to skirt hangers. (Clip over fabric to avoid marks on leather.) GH Institute tip: Keep the soles of hanging boots away from other hanging clothes.

GO HEEL TO TOE. Arrange shoes front to back. It gives you a speedy survey of color, toe style and heel height to help speed up getting dressed.

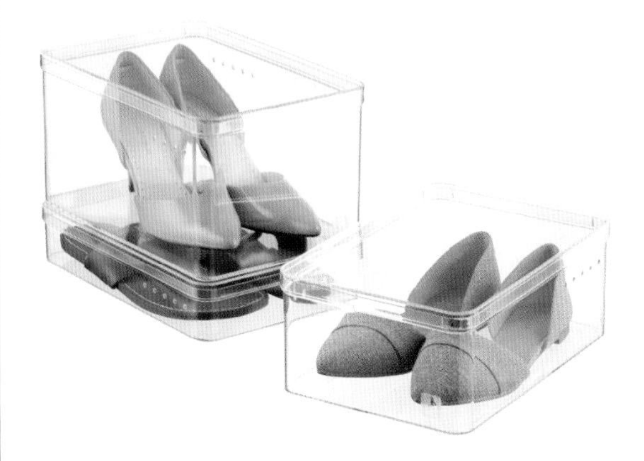

OPT FOR SEE-THROUGH BOXES. Your pieces will stay dust- and damage-free.

LIVE ON THE EDGE

While it may seem contradictory, sharp knives are actually safer to use than dull blades because they require less pressure to cut and don't slip as easily. For goof-proof sharpening, try GH Institute–tested Chef's Choice® ProntoPro Diamond Hone Knife Sharpener.

chapter

4

GOOD HOUSEKEEPING

KITCHEN HACKS

GO ABOVE AND BEYOND

Whether the issue is a lack of counter surfaces or no upper cabinets, installing a hanging rack above the work area is a sneaky way to maximize your storage space for frequently used tools and supplies.

hang a rack!
BOSCH
KitchenAid

GROW YOUR OWN

Raise your hand if you've bought herbs for a meal only to have the rest of the bunch go bad before you could use it. If this happens more than you'd like to admit, conserve food (and money) by planting several of your family's go-to seasonings. Snip as needed.

GET SPICY

To get your spice collection in order, replace dried herbs and spices every two years (at least). Buy spices you don't use frequently in smaller jars. Flip to page 79 for more ideas.

MAKE IT CLEAR

See-through jars are a pantry no-brainer: Knowing what you have on hand and how much saves you a trip to the market.

EXPAND YOUR WORKSPACE

For versatility, the only thing better than a built-in island is a non-built-in one. Opt for one with drawers to provide ample storage for cutlery, pots and baking supplies. Hang ladles or potholders from the sidebars. If space allows, add counter-height chairs so that family and friends can keep you company as you cook.

DECLUTTER THE KITCHEN

Stop fighting with the jumble of stuff in your cupboards and fridge—and streamline your cooking routine. Save a little money, too!

END THE LID AVALANCHE. Genius idea: Use a low-profile dish drainer to line up pot lids in a drawer. Drawers not deep enough? Look into nifty cabinet door-mount organizers.

PULL OUT. Difficult to see what's in the back of your cupboards? Retrofit them with slide-out shelves to access their recesses easily.

COMPARTMENTALIZE. Use slim trays and drawer dividers to neatly corral kitchen gadgets. An in-drawer knife block keeps blades sharp—and hidden from kids.

CLIP AND SAVE. Use clips to seal snacks, baking supplies or anything that could go stale quickly or attract pests. Clear dividers make items visible.

DE-STRESSED DINNER PREP

Make meal time easier—from the store to the kitchen.

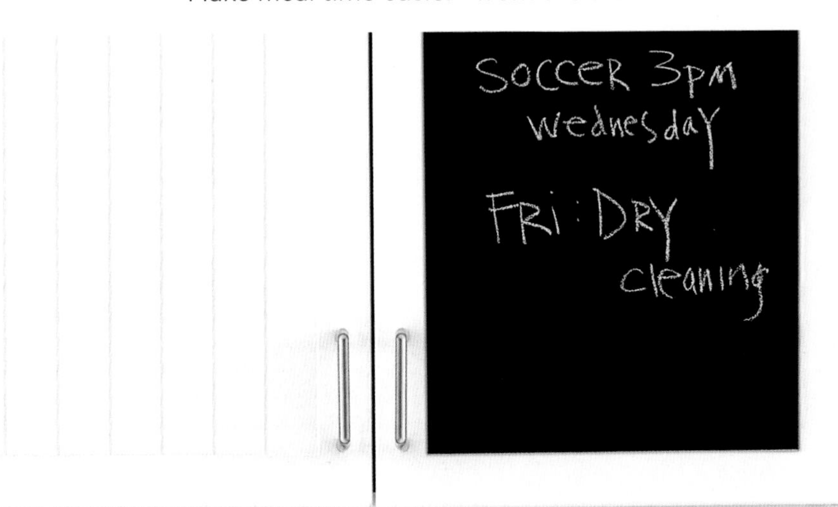

MAKE A MASTER LIST

Keep track of pantry supplies by listing items on a chalk or dry-erase board in the kitchen. Mark an X next to a food when you use the last of it; use this to make your list on shopping day (wipe off the Xs to start again). Or do it digitally: Instacart.com, a grocery delivery service, has a list-making feature that you can use even if you don't order groceries from them.

PLAN FOR UNPACKING

When loading food into the shopping cart and again when bagging at checkout, group items according to where they're stored at home—in the fridge, freezer or pantry. Harmful bacteria multiply at room temperature, so the quicker you can chill perishables, the better.

COOK AHEAD

Handle particularly busy nights by precooking meals. For instance, if you know your daughter's Girl Scout meeting is every Tuesday, prepare two meals on Monday nights—and store the second in airtight containers in the fridge. Or designate one Sunday a month for advance cooking.

SAVE $$$ AT THE

SUPER-MARKET

COUPONS

Every day, hundreds of printable grocery coupons are available on coupons.com, or you can load them onto its mobile app, Coupons.

KEYRING

Capitalize on your frequent-shopper status: Use the free Key Ring app to snag discounts and freebies at Safeway®, CVS®, Target®, Ralphs®, Trader Joe's® and more.

IBOTTA® AND CHECKOUT 51

Don't bother Instagramming your food—shoot your receipts instead! Free apps like Ibotta and Checkout 51 give you cash back for select items, as long as you upload a photo of the receipt as proof.

THE PERFECT PAN

Unlike your basic cookie sheet, which has only one or two curved sides for easier handling, a jellyroll pan has 1-inch-high sides. Perfect for making cake rolls, it can double as a cookie sheet or pizza stone and is terrific for roasting veggies, baking large batches of bar cookies or brownies and catching drips underneath bubbly casseroles and pies. You're welcome.

FAMILY MATTERS

An impressive 21 million children ages 17 and under watch the Food Network®. And Fox®'s *MasterChef Junior* and other shows now give them a TV avenue to show off their skills. Cooking together is a fun, affordable activity that can help kids gain key life skills. (Plus, not even a picky eater can resist tasting tilapia he herb-crusted himself!) Encourage your child to log favorite recipes in a spiral-bound "cookbook." She'll feel accomplished as she keeps track of her culinary creations.

THE SPICE IS RIGHT

Shelf risers or a tiered rack let you see all of your spices at a glance—so you'll cook with them more often. (DIY idea: Stack empty aluminum foil or plastic wrap boxes under spice jars to get the same effect.) Whenever you buy a new seasoning, add a small sticker to the bottle and write the purchase date on it.

KEEP FOOD FRESH LONGER

Follow these simple steps to make sure your food is safe and cut down on waste.

GIVE IT AIR

Don't overstuff your refrigerator—air needs room to circulate so that the appliance can work efficiently. The opposite is true with storage vessels: Fill containers almost to capacity, and remove as much air as possible from zip-seal bags or when wrapping items—in the fridge, freezer or on pantry shelves.

GO WITH THE GRAIN

Store grains and cereals in the fridge to preserve their freshness—particularly if you live in a warm climate. When it comes to bread, however, pop it in the freezer if you fear it may go stale or get moldy too soon (the fridge can dry it out). Toast or thaw as needed.

KEEP OR TOSS?

Set your fridge to 37°F, and follow these storage tips for food safety.

DAIRY & EGGS

Eggs: 3 to 5 weeks

Milk: 1 week

Butter: 1 to 3 months

Yogurt: 1 to 2 weeks

MEAT

Deli-sliced lunch meat: 3 to 5 days

Raw chicken or turkey: 1 to 2 days

Leftover cooked meat: 3 to 4 days

Raw ground meat: 1 to 2 days

FRUITS & VEGETABLES

Apples: 4 to 6 weeks

Citrus: 1 to 3 weeks

Berries: 7 to 10 days

Grapes: 1 week

Peppers: 4 to 14 days

Mushrooms: 3 to 7 days

Lettuce: 1 to 2 weeks

Corn on the cob: 1 to 2 days

CONDIMENTS

Mayonnaise: 2 months

Bottled salad dressing: 1 to 3 months

Ketchup: 6 months

CLEANING CHEATS

Minimize post-meal messiness in minutes.

STOVE-TOP TRICKS

Want to make stove-top cleaning easier? Cover adjoining burners with extra pot lids when sautéing. The lids are a much quicker cleanup than the burners. In the oven, if a spill happens, immediately and liberally sprinkle it with salt to soak up the liquid. When it cools, nudge the crusty stain loose with a spatula; wipe clean.

FULLY LOADED

The debate over the best way to load the dishwasher ends here. Follow these GH Institute–tested tips.

UTENSILS GO UP AND DOWN Forks: prongs up. Spoons: some up, some down to avoid nesting, which makes them harder to clean. Knives: blades down for safety.

FACE DISHES INWARD Load with the dirty sides facing the center, where the spray is the strongest.

STOP SPOTS Nestle glasses between tines—if they go over them, drops may dry where tines touch glasses; also, glasses can shift around and crack.

COMMON MISTAKE! Placing platters along the front of the bottom rack can interfere with the detergent being fully dispensed.

HAND-WASHING HOW-TO

1 To remove hard water deposits on nice glassware: Warm 2 cups of white vinegar in the microwave for two minutes and pour it into a plastic basin.

2 Place glasses, on their sides, in the vinegar. Soak for three minutes. Rotate as needed, so all surfaces of the glass are bathed in vinegar.

3 Rinse them in clear water and dry with a lint-free towel.

THAT'S GENIUS! Snag a **rubber glove** to help you get a grip on a stuck jar top.

THE PRETTY STUFF

You spend enough time in the kitchen; it ought to look nice.

CHIC AND CHEAP

Freestanding shelves are simpler (and less pricey) to put up than cabinets and give a breezy, casual feel to a kitchen. Open, slide-out shelves make cooking gear stashed in wicker easy to access.

SOOTHE THE PALETTE

An understated color scheme of soft grays and white turns your kitchen into a Zen retreat. Reflective finishes—polished marble floor, stainless steel appliances—make the room appear larger.

ADD A LITTLE POP

A cheery red banquette cushion invigorates the eating nook in the same kitchen. No built-in seating? Top chair seats with colorful cushions or drape the table with a bright cloth.

FOCUS ON CLEAN DESIGN

In a clutter-free kitchen, high-end touches—like brass knobs, a small chandelier and a marble mosaic backsplash—elevate everything around them. The matte black sink faucet seems sculptural when contrasted with the pale surroundings.

SOFTEN UP

The quickest low-cost way to change the look of your kitchen? Swap out the dish towels. (Extra credit: Update a cafe curtain over the sink.)

DOES IT PAY TO HIRE A PRO?

TO REFINISH CABINETS

If you're not known for your patience or precision, a professional cabinet makeover may be worth the splurge. After all, you have to remove the door and drawer fronts, be careful around cabinet lips and ledges and wait for each coat of paint or stain to dry. Basically it's not a simple weekend afternoon project.

However, if you've got a good dose of DIY spirit and a couple of days to spare, **Rust-Oleum® Cabinet Transformations®** makes it easy to get a custom look for less. Promising no stripping, sanding or priming plus no special skills required, the kit comes in two sizes, depending on the size of your cabinetry (100 or 200 square feet), and dozens of fresh finishes.

INSTANT WALL ART

Don't waste a scrap: Raid your sewing bin or hit the fabric store for coordinating samples. Showcase them in matching frames, hung in a grid for maximum impact.

chapter

5

GOOD HOUSEKEEPING

DECORATE IT YOURSELF

HEADBOARD REFRESH

To make over a lackluster headboard, grab a graphic woven rug, a sturdy rod, some rope and your toolbox. Hold the rod against the wall; drill two screws into the wall near each end, leaving ½ inch of each screw exposed. Wrap rope around the rod; hang on the screws. Drape your rug over top. Va-va-voom!

The Renaissance Garden in England
THE INQUISITOR'S HOUSE

ADD ARCHITECTURE

Living in a featureless box? Crown moulding along the ceiling or a chair rail around the center of the room lend character and style. Buy unfinished wood trim, cut it to fit your space, and then paint the pieces to match.

PEELING WALLPAPER

Put it back in its place with Red Devil's House & Home Restore™ Wallpaper Seam Repair. In GHI tests, it held up even in high humidity. Use the thin applicator to get behind raised seams; then press down gently for a minute and wipe off any excess.

HAVE HIGH IDEALS

Living in a place with low ceilings? Choose "short" furniture—pieces that are low and long (e.g., sofa, media cabinet, dresser). Together, they'll emphasize a horizontal line that's far from the ceiling, drawing the eye down so the space feels taller.

FOCUS ON THE FOYER

Painting this first-impression area a bold color gives you more bang for your buck. Why? Entryways tend to be smaller than, say, living rooms, so you won't need to cover so much square footage.

EASY ROOM MAKEOVERS

These speedy DIY solutions are totally worth the effort (and won't break the bank!).

REARRANGE THE FURNITURE

If your space's style has gone stale, try this free fix: Rearrange the furniture. But *before* you lift the sofa, consult a no-cost app like Home Design 3D to create a three-dimensional visualization. Then, go on and move pieces around at will.

DO THIS BRICK TRICK

Transform a dated redbrick fireplace with white or cream paint. Small accents—such as two turquoise vases on a coffee table or mantel—really pop against a pale backdrop.

ESTABLISH BORDER

Use an area rug to define a "room" in open space. And don't skimp on the carpet's size—one that's too small can shrink the zone. In the living room, make sure it's large enough so that the front legs of key furniture pieces are on it.

THAT'S GENIUS! Gently untangle fringe on carpets, upholstery and drapes as well as tasseled pulls with a **wide-toothed comb.**

GROWN-UP PASTELS

Why relegate these soft shades to kids' rooms? Sophisticated pastels—pale blue, yellow or green; pink, peach or lavender—lend serenity to your living spaces. Colored pillows and lamp shades are an affordable way to try a new scheme.

CAN'T-FAIL COLOR COMBOS

Designer trick: Look through your closet to determine which hues you prefer—and let them inspire your next decorating project. Here are a few that GH loves:

KELLY GREEN + GRAY Soft gray grounds feel-good green for a style that's at once earthy and energetic.

NAVY + TANGERINE Pops of tangy orange wake up classic navy. Layer in white for a casually crisp look.

TEAL + TAN Imagine sea glass nestled in beachy sand. This soothing palette is Mother Nature-made for decorating.

MAGENTA + RED Nothing packs a punch like vibrant hot pink. Well, nothing other than layering it with red.

PAINT A ROOM IN A DAY

Sample your shade (or several) in your space to see how it looks throughout the day. Then, follow these GH Institute–tested steps.

1 **COVER UP.** Use fabric drop cloths to protect the floor and any furniture from paint splatters and spills.

2 **CLEAN FIRST.** Paint won't adhere as well to a dirty surface, so first use a microfiber sweeper to remove dust, cobwebs and soot from the walls. Swab down extra-grimy parts with a wet sponge or cloth; let dry.

3 **PATROL THE BORDERS.** Remove outlet and light-switch covers, and tape off any areas you don't want painted.

4 **PICK YOUR PAINT.** Use one with a built-in primer, like Benjamin Moore® Aura®, to cover a dark wall with a light color in a fraction of the time (thanks to fewer coats). Going from light to light? Two coats of good-quality regular paint should do it.

5 **START IN THE CORNERS.** With an angled brush, paint a 2-inch border around taped-off areas as well as the ceiling. Then, fill in the central unpainted space using a paint tray and roller in overlapping W- or M-shaped strokes. Let the first coat dry for at least a couple of hours, then coat again. Have a moist rag handy to wipe fresh splatters.

6 **FINISH UP.** Rinse your paintbrush and roller under a faucet until the water runs clear. Decant the tray's leftover paint back into the can; seal the can tightly. Rinse your tray or throw away the liner.

7 **LEAVE NO TRACE.** Scrape off dried drips with a credit card or plastic spatula. Remove painter's tape before you call it a night, pulling it off at an angle to avoid tearing the finish.

GOTTA HAVE 'EM! PAINTING ESSENTIALS

Don't start your project without this gear.

PAINTER'S TAPE

Painter's tape protects moldings, baseboards and window frames, and comes off more easily than regular masking tape.

ANGLED BRUSH

Pick up a 2-inch angled brush for the best control when edging around ceilings and taped areas.

PAINT TRAY AND PLASTIC LINERS

Do you *really* need liners? Only if you want to deal with a *lot* less mess! You can even ball up and throw out Peel-a-Tray liners when you're done.

FABRIC DROP CLOTH

Choose a canvas cover instead of plastic. The latter can be slick under your feet.

ROLLER COVER

The wrong nap will apply too much or too little paint. Use this rule of thumb: Look for one with a ¼-inch nap for smooth surfaces, ⅜-inch for semi-smooth or ⅝-inch for rough or textured.

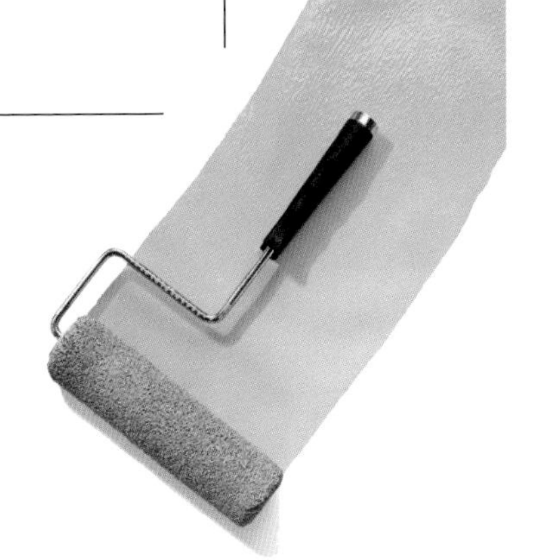

ROLLER FRAME AND EXTENSION POLE

The roller frame is what your cover slips onto. For easier detachment, try a quick-release frame-handle holder by Shur-Line®. Another worthy investment: a pro-style Purdy® extension pole.

MAKE SMALL SPACES LIVE LARGER

Maximize your square footage—or at least its appearance—without changing addresses.

ADD NATURAL ELEMENTS

Fresh bouquets and botanical prints as well as wicker baskets and a sisal area rug all blur the distinction between the indoors and out. Use them throughout small rooms—or your entire house—to keep from feeling hemmed in.

TRICK OUT TIGHT CORNERS

Mount a clever corner ledge above a door to display candles or other decorative touches. Similarly, freestanding or built-in corner cabinets can make all the difference in storage-starved bathrooms, entryways and kitchens.

DIVVY IT UP

Open floor plans are more spacious, right? Not necessarily. A cavernous room can become a chaotic waste of space unless you establish inviting zones. Divide one into separate rooms with an open-back bookcase that's half-filled.

SOFT TOUCHES

Want your rooms to say, "Come in and stay awhile"?
Layer on the fabric accents.

DRAPE YOURSELF IN STYLE

Beyond their intended purposes (e.g., controlling outdoor light, regulating indoor temperatures and, you know, providing a little privacy), floor-to-ceiling drapes draw the eye up, which makes your room seem taller. If your home gets a lot of sunlight, select a fade-proof fabric like Sunbrella® for your curtains.

ADD SOME PADDING

Are you and your partner on different ends of the how-many-pillows-should-be-on-the-bed spectrum? Compromise with an upholstered headboard. A rectangular or camelback style in a neutral hue offers classy cushiness, while one in a dramatic silhouette, color or pattern becomes a bold focal point.

PATTERN PLAY

Show some personality with prints. It's the decorating equivalent of letting your hair down.

ESTABLISH PRIORITIES

Let a bold wallpaper be the star of the show. Keep additional artwork sparse and simple: A small collection of gilded frames, for example, won't overpower the paper's design. Likewise, unfussy furniture—a clean-lined table, clear acrylic chairs—don't compete with your primary pattern.

KEEP YOUR BALANCE

The number one rule for layering patterns? Stay in the same color palette. Start with a wow-factor print that sets the tone, like a bold zigzag or a bright abstract. Find a fabric that echoes the colors in your main pattern but features smaller-scale prints. Add a stripe, a check or a solid, and you're officially a mix master!

GO SMALL

Not ready to commit to all-over prints? Not to worry. Even a dash of a vibrant repeat has major impact against a blank background—think orange or yellow chevron-patterned pillows on a white sofa. Another solution: Keep your patterns soft and neutral (e.g., gray and white, tan and cream) to add subtle visual texture.

CURATE YOUR COLLECTIONS

First, edit out those not-so-favorite things, then arrange the keepers in style. You'll love them that much more.

BRIGHTEN WITH BOOKS

Bibliophiles, rejoice: Now your collection of beloved hardcovers and yellowed paperbacks can serve a second purpose—as handy decorating tools. Simply group your different genres by spine shade. The effect? A hit of color as pretty as a painting.

INSPIRE THE SCHEME

Celebrate everyday objects like graphic-print plates—they'll stand out against basic, uncluttered bookshelves. While you're at it, why not use their colors throughout the room? Here, hardwood floors are stained a leafy green to match.

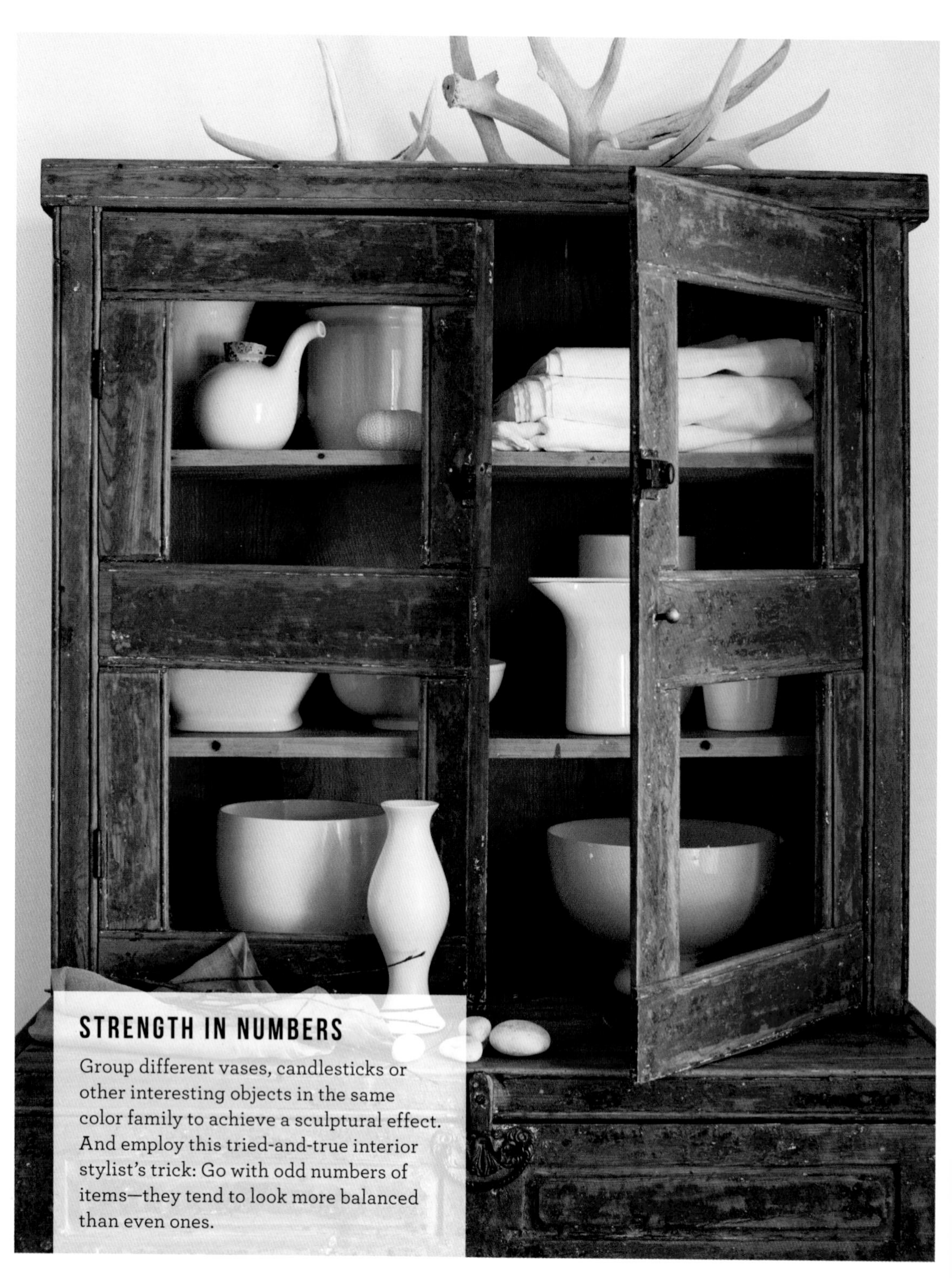

STRENGTH IN NUMBERS

Group different vases, candlesticks or other interesting objects in the same color family to achieve a sculptural effect. And employ this tried-and-true interior stylist's trick: Go with odd numbers of items—they tend to look more balanced than even ones.

CASH IN!

TURN OLD FURNITURE INTO $$$

Sure, you could have a killer tag sale, but there are easier—and more profitable—ways to pocket some green.

On **CRAIGSLIST**® and **EBAY**®, brand names in like-new condition usually bring in bigger bucks (Pottery Barn® tables, KitchenAid mixers), but items from another era (e.g., china pieces produced from a limited run) are also in demand.

FACEBOOK® "yard sale" themed groups bring together buyers and sellers: Post a photo of the item for sale, and friends in your group will see it. Interested buyers contact you via the comments page or private message.

REPLACEMENTS, LTD.®, buys china, crystal and flatware from anywhere in the United States. Once you receive a quote, ship it to them: If they like what they see, they'll pay within a week; if they don't, they'll return it free of charge.

CHAIRISH is a stylish buy-and-sell site for design aficionados. But don't be discouraged if you don't have a spare Barcelona® chair to hawk. The site also accepts "non-branded items with great character." It's free to list, and you'll make 80 percent on any sale.

TOP-DOLLAR TRICK

Reveal what the item you're selling is going for at retail now—along with what you paid for it way back when. This may put the asking price in a better light.

PHOTO CREDITS

COVER PHOTOGRAPHY: timeincukcontent: front; Mark Lund: back cover top; Victoria Pearson: back cover bottom

INTERIOR PHOTOGRAPHY: ©Antonis Achilleos: 31; ©Lucas Allen: 73; ©Courtney Apple: 22, 104; ©Burcu Avsar: 39; Jesus Ayala/Studio D: 63; ©James Baigrie: 9; ©Stacy Bass: 97; courtesy of Bella Storage Solution: 39; ©Ryan Benyi: 57; ©Stacey Brandford: 85, 86, 92, 94, 107; ©Liz Clayman Photography: 68; courtesy of ClosetMaid: 62; courtesy of The Container Store: 51, 60, 67; ©Mike Daines/Photoshot: 18; depositphotos.com: ©Dessie_bg: 65; Ha4ipiri: 67; kitchbain: 83; courtesy of Eau Palm Beach Resort and Spa: 103; Chris Eckert/Studio D: 99; ©Don Freeman: 24; Philip Freidman/Studio D: 39, 43, 65, 83, 99; ©Dana Gallagher: 17, 29, 32; ©Mike Garten: 63, 72, 97; Getty Images: Colin Anderson: 12; Alistair Berg: 19; Fotografia Inc.: 17; Lus Ferraz/Eye Em: 82; Fuse: 21; Mike Harrington: 16; Alex Hayden: 20; Paula Hible/Food Pix: 11; Jupiterimages: 98; Mark Lund: 61; mollypix: 83; Jeremy Samuelson: 53; Howard Shooter: 51; Angela Wyatt: 8; Ben Goldstein/Studio D: 99, 109; iStock: Acerebel: 59; adlifemarketing: 21; Anne Clark: 17; davidoff777: 81; DmitiriMaruta: 21; Floortje: 81; gavran333: 78; John Gollop: 59; Izabela Habur: 65; IPGGutenbergUKLtd: 77; JazzIRT: 14; JestersCap: 17; jwblinn: 83; macniak: 65; Margorious: 109; misscherrygolightly: 13; Olezzo: 13; omersukrugoksu: 77; Dominik Pabis: 15; sf_foodphoto: 78; thisisaghosttown: 13; unalozmen: 109; YinYang: 80; Devon Jarvis/Studio D: 63; courtesy of LG: 83; Loupe Images: @Simon Brown: 93; ©Polly Wreford: 28, 101; courtesy of Link: 67; ©Mark Lund: 4,31, 38, 52, 55, 76, 97, 105; courtesy of Mary McDonald for Schumacher: 105; ©Andrew McCaul: 13, 26,30, 33, 37, 48, 49, 54, 56, 59, 66; Marko Metzinger/Studio D: 39; ©Ellie Miller: 79; ©Keith Scott Morton: 7; J Muckle/Studio D: 95; ©Wendi Nordeck: 44; ©Victoria Pearson: 84; ©David Prince: 36; Lara Robby/Studio D: 9, 27; ©Lisa Romerein: 88, 102; ©Paul Ryan-Goff: 6; ©Annie Schlechter: 70; courtesy of Serena and Lily: 97; courtesy of Shur-Line: 99; Shutterstock: Africa Studio: 34, 35, 64; Adam Fillipowicz: 109; imging: 21; iofoto: 99; Pixel-Shot: 50; courtesy of Anna Sigga/www.scrappalicious.com: 45; Kevin Sweeney/Studio D: 59, 63, 67; ©Kat Teutsch: 90; timeincukcontent.com: 42, 96; ©David Tsay: 87; courtesy of Umbra: 39; ©Bjorn Wallander: 10, 46, 108; ©Monica Wang: 100, 101; ©Wendell T. Webber: 58; ©courtesy of West Elm: 39; ©courtesy of Williams-Sonoma Home: 74; ©Anthea Williamson: 106; ©Brian Woodcock: 41; ©Reven T.C. Wurman Photography: 95; ©Jonny Valiant: 40; ©Jim Wright: 75

INDEX

Ammonia, 17, 18, 19

Baskets for storage, 24, 39, 40, 41, 46, 100
Bathroom
  container control, 30
  organizing storage, 30
  speed-cleaning tips, 15, 17
  toilet bowl cleaner recipe, 17
Bedroom. *See also* Closets, organizing
  accessory organization ideas, 66, 67
  headboard refresh, 90–91
  surface-top organization, 28
Bleach
  ammonia mix precaution, 18
  cleaning kitchen sponge with, 21
  for fabrics, 10
  for toilet bowl cleaner, 17
Books, storing, 31, 36, 101, 106
Bread, storing, 81
Brick fireplace, painting, 94

Candles and candlesticks, 101
Carpets and rugs
  area rugs to define "room," 95
  cleaning, 11, 20
  machines for cleaning, 11, 21
  minimizing dirt on, 6
  stain-removal tips, 20
  untangling fringe on, 95
  vacuums for, 21
Cars, washing, 19
Cedar, moths and, 65
Cleaning, 4–21. *See also* Kitchen, cleaning
  chores, divvying up, 16
  dish towels, 7
  don'ts, 18–19
  floors, 6
  paper towels for, 9

portable paper towel dispenser for, 9
smart cleaning tips, 8–9
speed-cleaning tips, 14–17
supplies. *See* Cleaning tools and supplies
using less product, 9
windows, 7, 9
Cleaning tools and supplies
caring for, 21
homemade cleaner recipes, 17
paper towels, 9
vacuum cleaners, 21
Clips, to seal things with, 75
Closets, organizing
accessories, 66, 67
custom design tips, 60–62
hangers, 41
hanging bins/totes, 66
hanging vs. folding clothes, 61
linen closet, 26
mothproofing tips, 65
on-door hanging pockets, 38, 48
professional help, 45
removing door for access, 60
Clothing care, 46–67. *See also* Closets, organizing; Laundry
airtight containers, 65
drawer scent ideas, 49
dressing preparation, 48
hangers, 67
hanging vs. folding, 61
ironing, avoiding wrinkles, 55
mending essentials, 58–59
mothproofing tips, 65
organizing drawers, 49
sewing kit for, 58–59
stain-removal tips, 50, 65
Clothing, selling or donating, 63–64
Clutter, removing. *See* Organizing
Coffee beans, for odors, 12
Coffee stains, removing, 50
Collections, 106–108
Color
can't-fail combos, 97
grouping collections by, 108
painting guidelines and supplies, 98–99
painting redbrick fireplaces, 94
pastels, 96
Condiments, storing, 81
Countertops. *See* Kitchen countertops
Crown moulding, 92

Dairy, storing, 81
Decorating, 88–109. *See also* Color
adding natural elements, 100
collections, 106–108
corner ledge above door, 101
defining/dividing rooms, 95, 101
entryways, 6, 93
fabric accents, 102–103
headboard refresh, 90–91
instant wall art, 88
kitchen design tips, 84–87
offsetting low-ceiling effects, 93
painting guidelines and supplies, 98–99
painting redbrick fireplaces, 94
pattern play, 104–105
rearranging furniture, 94
small spaces, 93, 100–101
trim and crown moulding, 92
wallpaper repair, 92
Desk, organizing, 33–35
Dishes, washing, 83
Dish towels, 7, 87
Doors
mats by, 6
removing from closet, 60
storage pockets hanging on, 38, 48
Drapes, 102
Drawers
clothing, 49
junk, reclaiming, 31
kitchen, 74, 75
liners, 49
organizing, 31, 44, 49, 75
pull-out, 75
Drying clothes, 53–54

Eggs, storing, 81
Entryways, decorating, 6, 93

Fabric accents, 102–103
drapes, 102
pillows, 96, 103, 105
wall art, 88
Fireplace, painting, 94
Floors. *See also* Carpets and rugs
cleaning, 19
doormats on, 6
removing shoes before walking on, 6
Fruits, storing, 81
Furniture
cleaning tip, 10
old, selling, 109
rearranging, 94
slip covers, 10
streamlining, 29

Gift wrap, organizing, 27
Glassware, washing, 83
Grocery shopping, 76–77
Growing, herbs, 72

Hangers, 41, 67
Herbs and spices, organizing, 73, 79
Herbs, growing, 72
Hooks, 28, 39, 41, 43, 48
Hydrogen peroxide, 17

Ironing/wrinkle-removal tips, 55, 61

Kitchen, 68–87
cabinet refinishing, 87
chalkboard-painted wall, 22
color tips, 85, 87
cooking ahead, 77
cooking with kids/family, 78
design tips, 84–87
dish towels, 7, 87
expanding workspace, 74
growing herbs, 72
keeping food fresh, 79, 80–81
life spans of various foods, 81
lighting, 86
meal-prep tips, 76–77
pans for. *See* Pots and pans
refrigerators, 14, 80
restocking tips, 76–77
sharpening knives, 68
Kitchen, cleaning
dishes, 83
dish towels, 7, 87
dishwasher prep and load, 16, 83
don'ts, 18, 19
lemon-fresh microwave and disposal, 11
refrigerator, 14
speed-cleaning tips, 14, 16, 17
stove-top and oven, 82
Kitchen countertops
cleaning, 17, 18
lack of, solutions, 70
Kitchen organization
clutter control tips, 37, 75
drawer dividers/trays, 75
food-saver tips, 79, 80–81
herbs and spices, 73, 79

Kitchen organization *(continued)*
- lids storage, 37, 75
- meal prep and, 76–77
- open shelving, 84
- pantry, 73, 76
- portable island for, 74
- slide-out shelves, 75, 84
- tracking supplies, 76
- wall racks, 70–71

Knives, sharpening, 68

Laundry
- drying, 53–54, 57
- gentle detergent recipe, 17
- ironing, avoiding wrinkles, 55
- preparing for, 50
- protecting delicates (undies, bras, etc.), 56–57
- room organization, 46, 55
- sorting, 51
- stain-remover recipe, 17
- time-saving tips, 8, 50–52
- wash cycles, 52, 60

Lemons, fresh scent from, 11
Lighting, kitchen, 86
Linen closet, organizing, 26
Linens, drying, 53
Living room
- easy makeovers, 94–96
- organization tips. *See* Clutter, removing; Organizing
- streamlining furniture, 29

Meat, storing, 81
Mothproofing tips, 65
Mudroom, organizing, 40–43

Newspapers
- organizing, 17

Odor elimination
- coffee beans for, 12
- lemons for, 11

Organizing. *See also* Closets, organizing; Kitchen organization
- baskets for, 24, 39, 40, 41, 46, 100
- bathroom storage/countertop, 30
- boxes/trays for, 29, 39
- desk, 33–35
- gift wrap, bags, etc., 27
- hiring professional help, 45
- hooks for, 28, 39, 41, 43, 48
- jewelry, 28
- junk drawer, 31
- labeling items, 45
- laundry room, 46
- lazy Susans for, 39
- mudroom, 40–43
- preventing paper clutter, 32–35
- rules of thumb, 28, 44–45
- speed-cleaning/organizing tips, 17
- under stairs, 42
- suitcases for, 24
- tricks that work, 28-31
- vertical surfaces for, 36–38
- vessels, creative ideas, 24

Oven, cleaning, 82

Painting
- guidelines for, 98
- paint recommendations, 98
- redbrick fireplace, 94
- supplies for, 99

Paper clutter, preventing, 32–35
Paper shredders, 35
Paper towel dispenser, portable, 9
Patterns, decorating tips, 104–105
Pets
- de-fuzzing fur deposits, 13
- de-stinking between baths, 13
- preventing food/water spills, 13
- stain-removal tips, 13, 20
- urine cleanup/deterrent, 13

Pillows, 96, 103, 105
Plate collection, 106–108
Pots and pans, 78

Refrigerators, 14, 80
Rugs. *See* Carpets and rugs
Rust stains, 18

Selling
- old clothes, 63
- old furniture, 109

Sharpening knives, 68
Shelving
- closet, 60–62
- for collections, 106–108
- corner ledge above door, 101
- decor tip, 31
- floor-to-ceiling, 36
- kitchen, 84
- laundry room, 46, 55
- for organizing, 36
- organizing rules, 44
- risers, for spices, 79
- slide-out, 75
- under stairs, 42

Shoes, organizing, 67
Shoes, removing in house, 6
Shower, cleaner recipe, 17
Shredding papers, 35
Small spaces, decorating, 93, 100–101
Spices, organizing, 73, 79
Stains
- carpet, 20
- clothing/fabric, 50, 65
- drawer liners causing, 49
- on hard surfaces (pans, stoves, etc.), 82
- household cleaners for, 50
- laundry, 17
- pet urine, 13
- rust, 18

Storage. *See* Closets, organizing; Kitchen organization; Organizing
Stove-top, cleaning, 82
Suitcases, vintage organizers, 24

Tools, for cleaning. *See* Cleaning tools and supplies
Trim and crown moulding, 92

Urine, pet, 13

Vacuum cleaners, 21
Vegetables, storing, 81
Vinegar
- cleaning glassware with, 83
- precautions for using, 18, 19

Wallpaper
- bold, featuring, 104
- covering backs of shelves with, 31
- repairing peeling, 92

Washing clothes. *See* Laundry
Windows
- cleaner recipe, 17
- cleaning, 7, 9

Wrinkles, removing/avoiding (fabric), 55
Wrinkles, removing (fabric), 61
Wrinkles, removing (gift bags/ribbons), 27